" DARLINGHURST NIGHTS—*!*"

Darlinghurst Nights

and Morning Glories
Being 47 strange sights
  Observed from eleventh storeys,
In a land of cream puffs and crime,
  By a Flat-roof Professor;
And here set forth in sketch and rhyme

by

"VIRGIL"
and
KENNETH SLESSOR

ETT IMPRINT, SYDNEY

This edition published by ETT Imprint 2015

ETT IMPRINT
PO Box R1906
Royal Exchange NSW 1225
Australia

First published by Frank Johnson 1933. Published by
Angus & Robertson 1981. Published by ETT Imprint 2015.

ISBN 978-1-925416-06-0 pbk
ISBN 978-1-925416-07-7 eBook

The author is grateful to Smith's Weekly, who first published
these verses and drawings in their newspaper.

Design by Hanna Gotlieb

CONTENTS

DELICATESSEN

Little, round cherries in little, round
  glasses,
  Oysters in bottles, and soup a la can,
Over the counter, the grocery passes,
  All for the love of a man—
All for the sake of some far-away someone.
  Chafing with hunger in far-away state,
Snatching from Mammon a mouthful of
  salmon,
  Banging a fork on his plate.

Still is the pistol of Smith and of Wesson,
  Stilled is the wish of the gunman to roam,
Delicatessen, delicatessen,
  Delicatessen, come home!

Ladies who linger too late with a bargain,
  Chaffeurs whose mistresses peer from their cars,
All down the counter, they crowd with their
  jargon
  Buying their dinner in jars;
Food for the flat, and a snack for the wealthy,

Arrogant truffles and vulgar sardines,
  Herrings and custard and mushrooms and mus-
    tard,
      Caviar, chicken, and beans.

Vain is the lore of the cookery-lesson,
  Faced by the fangs of a ravenous male—
Delicatessen, delicatessen,
  Delicatessen for sale!

Ham, pink as roses, and peaches and pickles,
  Onions in crystal, like globules of gold,
Out of the window, the treasury trickles,
  Greedily, speedily sold;
Olives and gherkins and sauerkraut and white
    bait,
  Pork and asparagus, captive in tin—
Searching for any marked "Tasty, One Penny,"
  Faces gaze wistfully in.

Misting the glass of the windows they press on.
  Snub, little noses pushed flat with a sigh—
Delicatessen, delicatessen,
  Delicatessen, good-bye!

Country Eyes

Diana is down from the station,
A fortnight from Heaven-Knows-Where—
Her favorite hobby is down in the lobby
  With gratification
  To sit in a chair.

The lords and the ladies, the beautiful ladies,
The lords and the ladies are noble to see,
In sables and satins, they tinkle Manhattans
Or dabble their diamonds in butter and tea.

The music is always by Tosti,
  Delightfully wicked and gay;
Each waiter that passes has 500 glasses,
  All pink, green, and frosty,
  That shine on his tray.

And the lords and the ladies, the sweet, pretty ladies,
The lords and the ladies take supper in sips,
In satins and sables at little round tables,
With little round cocktails and little round lips.

And Spanish ambassadors linger
  In elegant gloom with their beer—
Magnificent creatures with classical features—
While twiddling one finger,
  There's Cuthbert de Vere!

But the lords and the ladies, the wonderful ladies,
The lords and the ladies look round in surprise—
Mouth open, heart beating, too breathless for eating
Diana sits watching with shining great eyes.

The lords have a habit of lying,
  The archdukes are out of a job,
The frolicsome ladies are Cohens and Gradys,
  And Cuthbert is dying
  To borrow two bob.

All the touts at their tables, the middle-aged Mabels
The second-hand butterflies, mumble and peer;
The Dresden princesses have dirt on their dresses.
Diana is twenty—Romance is so near!

Virgil

The Green Rolls Royce

Where the iceman doesn't cater
    For the idle millionaire
With his private Kelvinator
    And his faithful Frigidaire,
Where the windows gleam with
        money
    And the wine is never sly,
And the world is always sunny
    And the rent is always high,
And the landlord says with passion
    The locality is "choice,"
In a condescending fashion
    Goes the green Rolls Royce.

Where the Black Marias clatter,
    And peculiar ladies nod,
And the flats are rather flatter,
    And the lodgers rather odd,
Where the night is full of dangers
    And the darkness full of fear,
And eleven hundred strangers
    Live on aspirin and beer,
Where the gas-lights flare and flutter
    And the phonographs rejoice,
Like an archduke in the gutter
    Goes the green Rolls Royce.

If you care to do some prying,
    And you want to get some thrills,
You can hear a lady sighing
    To a pocketful of bills:

"Here's the rent-day getting closer,
    I can't bear things as they are,
You will have to pay the grocer
    Or I'll have to sell the car."
But no sooner has she said it
    In a melancholy voice,
Than she goes and gets some credit
    With the green Rolls Royce.

The Tiger in the Rose

Rosie at the Stadium
  Flaunts around her neck
Rubies rare as radium,
  Diamonds by the peck;
Furs of real peschaniki,
  Staggering the Press,
Make the neighbours panicky
  Not in evening dress.
Rosie's not the simple little angel you suppose,
Down behind a dimple there's a Tiger
             in
                the
                  Rose!

Eyes like infant violets
  Shine in Rosie's face,
Serenades and triolets
  Hang around the place,
Talk of possibilities,
  Pansies in a rage—
Once they start hostilities,
  Rosie goes Stone Age.
Shouting all the louder,"Paste him on the nose!"
Underneath the powder, there's a Tiger
             in
                the
                  Rose!

Jungle creatures loitering
  Down in Rosie's heart,
Leap out reconnoitring
  When the fighters start;
Fairies love ferocity—
  Rosie starts to shout,
Filled with animosity,
  "Bust him on the snout!"
Never mind the posy, disregard the pose,
Have a look at Rosie! There's a Tiger
             in
                the
                  Rose!

CHOKER'S LANE

In Choker's Lane, the doors appear
  Like black and shining coffin-lids,
Whose fill of flesh, long buried here,
  Familiar visiting forbids.

But sometimes, when their bells are
    twirled,
  They'll show, like Hades, through
    the chink,
The green and watery gaslight
    world
  Where girls have faces white as
    zinc.

And sometimes thieves go smoothly
    past,
  Or pad by moonlight home again,
For even thieves come home at last,
  Even the thieves of Choker's Lane.

And sometimes you can feel the
    breath
  Of beasts decaying in their den—
The soft, unhurrying teeth of Death
  With leather jaws come tasting
    men.

Then sunlight comes, the tradesmen nod,
  The pavement rings with careless feet,
And Choker's Lane—how very odd!—
  Is just an ordinary street.

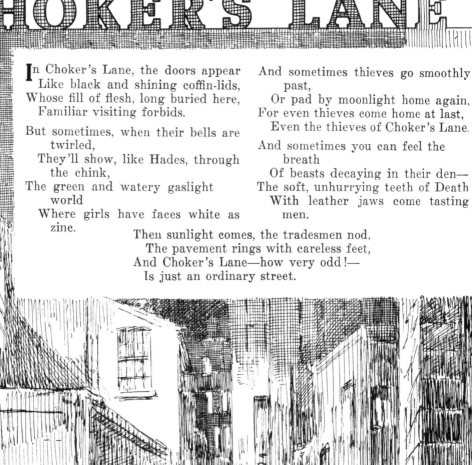

The Voice on the Wire

If angels could speak on a city exchange,
  Or fairies blow flutes in the battery,
I wouldn't consider your murmur so strange
  Nor choke the receiver with flattery,
But Postmaster-Generals frown at the flute,
  And angels don't argue with Nemesis,
One memo. from Kitto makes nightingales mute
  And fairies are warned off the premises.

    Oh, Mr. Jones, you do say things!
      It's breaking regulations,
    And every time your number rings
      You start these conversations,
    The monitor gets so enraged,
      It's very aggravating.
    What's that? No, madam. Line's engaged.
      Twopence, please. Waiting. Waiting.

I'd pay ninety guineas, not 2d. a call,
  If only I had the felicity
To carry you off, with your headphones and all,
  Away from accursed electricity,
To carry you off like a sylph of the air,
  Away on a magic trajectory,
Where bells never ring, and subscribers
  don't swear,
  And nobody owns a directory.

    Oh, Mr. Jones, you've got a nerve,
      I've wasted time already.
    It's really more than you deserve.
      The idea! Call you Freddy?
    You keep your fancies to the
      'phone,
    It's years since I've been
      carried.
  I'm 39, eleven stone,
    And, Mr. Jones, I'm married.

KIMONO CORA

Kimono Cora, she's like an aurora,
  She blazes with bangles of brass,
She wears a pearl necklace, her rubies are reckless
  (You'd never suspect they were glass).
The tramguards look round as she leaps from the ground,
  The taximen yearn as they pass,
The passengers stiffen, so sheer is her chiffon,
  She brandishes such an extent—
All stockings and singlet, two shoes and a ringlet,
  She's covered with satin and scent.

    Kimono Cora, Kimono Cora,
      Kimono Cora's in town.
    She knows how to speak like a thousand
        a week,
      But she frequently hasn't a brown.
    Well, diamonds can roll in the gutter,
      And lilies can blossom in grime,
    But no one supposes that attar of roses
      Can grow out of potage de slime.

Kimono Cora has such a plethora
  Of dashing society friends,
But, gossip or lover, they never discover
  The stairway that Cora ascends.
She waves them goodbye with a spark of the eye,
  Then—suddenly—everything ends.
No longer the flapper, she flings on a wrapper
  Bedraggled with ages of dirt,
Sour perfume still lingers, there's grime on her fingers,
  And grease on the edge of her skirt . . .

    Kimono Cora, Kimono Cora,
      Kimono Cora's come back,
    To her dirt and her debts and her stale cigarettes,
      And a pile of foul plates in her track
    Well, stars are reflected in quagmires,
      And wines don't depend on the cup,
    And Cora emerges in satins and serges
      From mystery—seven floors up!

Carmen of the Chorus

When Carmen capers floating
  So dangerously nice,
The stalls are full of doting,
  The boxes full of Zeiss.
In thistledown defiance
  Her rosy ankles twist—
O, Limbs that baffle science,
  O, Curves that Euclid missed!

Carmen of the Chorus, scandalously simple.

Her brain is partly porous, but she waves a
  wicked dimple;
She may be rather silly, as chorus-ladies go.
But she dances like a lily
                in the Very
                      Front
                            Row!

As eight o'clock is jangling,
  Her feet in pirouettes
Are punctually dangling
  Their golden pantalettes.

The noblest leg in drama
  Kicks wisdom to the heights—
O, Princess of Pyjama,
  O, Pretty One in Tights!
Let them sneer and snigger and classify
  geraniums,
  YOU possess a Figure, which is more
    than clever craniums;
Professors are all crazy, as most prof-
  essors know,
  And could THEY dance like a daisy
      In the Very
            FARTHEST
                  Row?

The Girl in the Window

The girl in the window
  Looks over the square
At a girl in a window
  With pearls in her hair,
With diamonds to dangle
  And feathers to preen,
A comb and a bangle,
  As proud as a queen,
In a flat so becoming,
  So silken and sleek,
With hot and cold plumbing
  (Ten guineas a week),
Where life is no harder
  For paying a price,
With fowls in the larder
  And Heidsieck on ice.
No need to be thrifty
  Or spend and repent,
With "Papa" aged fifty
  To fix up the rent.

    The girl in the window
      Looks over the square
    And sees, in a mirror,
      Herself standing there!

The girl in the window
  Looks over the square
At a girl in a window
  With eyes of despair,
In a cheap little attic,
  A cheap little dress,
All cotton and Batik
  (Ten shillings or less),
A trunk with no label,
  A ricketty bed,
A broken-down table,
  A banquet of bread,
The wallpaper peeling,
  A crack in the door,
Dirt on the ceiling,
  And dust on the floor;
No hope for to-morrow,
  The money all spent,
A fortnight of sorrow
  Behind in the rent.

    The girl in the window
      Looks over the square
    At a girl in a window—
      Herself!—standing there.

IT, IF and ALSO!

When skyscrapers burst into lilac,
    And Burgundy foams by the tank,
And nightingales carol their joy by the barrel,
    Or nest in the Commonwealth Bank;
When constables faint upon duty,
    And 'buses collide with a sigh—
By tokens of similar beauty,
    You'll know that it's Clara—
          Adorable Clara—
The Girl who has IT passing by.

What makes the tram-guard turn his
    head,
    What makes the traffic stall so?
You can follow in a daze to investi-
    gate her ways,
    She's the Girl who added IF and
    ALSO!

Like Venus disguised in a jumper,
    She brightens the dingiest home,
With charm and chinchilla converting a villa
    To Somebody's Palace at Rome.
Her followers never diminish,
    Her manners, you've got to admit,
Improve the original Glynnish
    By adding Conjunctions—
          Important Conjunctions—
    By adding Conjunctions to IT.

What wins the simple
    millionaire?
    What makes the peerage
    fall so?
It's the wisdom and the wit,
    and the little bit of IT,
And the IF
    and the HOW
        and the ALSO!

Gardens in the Sky

There's a golden hocus-pocus
    Where the buried people eat,
For the air is full of crocus
    Blowing down to William Street—
Oh, behold the Roman candles
    Of the window-boxes burst,
As the fairies tap their sandals
    On the Alps of Darlinghurst!

Everywhere, everywhere, flowers are fleeting in the air,
Lovers greeting, poets meeting, flowers are fleeting
                everywhere.

Where the stars are lit by Neon,
    Where the fried potato fumes,
And the ghost of Mr. Villon
    Still inhabits single rooms,
And the girls lean out from heaven
    Over lightwells, thumping mops,
While the gent in 57
    Cooks his pound of mutton chops—

Even there, even there, flowers are floating in the air;
Eyes are gloating, boarders doting, flowers are floating
                even there.

With a teacup full of water
    And a proud possessive eye,
You can see the landlord's daughter
    Damping gardens in the sky;
While her parent, having planted
    Half-a-yard of daffodils
(Is the butter-box enchanted?)
    Mows the lawn on window-sills.

Up the stair, down the stair, flowers are flying every-
           where;
  Birds are crying. bailiffs sighing. flowers are flying
                here
              and
                there!

Ticket In Tatts!

Ride a Blue Cab to the top of King's Cross,
Don't mind the money, don't think of the loss,
  Three cheers for Flemington,
  Bah to the Remington,
Farewell to Pitman, good-bye to the boss,
No more dictation and no more comptometers,
Blow up the office and burn the chronometers,
Buy a few diamonds and price a few hats,
Flaunt a few furs and inspect a few flats,
  No more economy,
  Here's to gastronomy!
Daisy's won—how much?

                              FIVE
                                THOUSAND
                                    IN TATTS!

Farewell finances that wrinkle the brow,
Good-bye to trams, we use Cadillacs now,
  Hickory, dickory,
  Gas-rings and chicory,
Watch us drink nothing but Moet—and how!
Bring out your truffles, we'll dine upon venison,
Smile at Sir Samuel, hobnob with Denison,
Flirt with George Cohen in ten-guinea hats,
Fox-trot with no one who doesn't wear spats—
  In a kind of paralysis,
  Picturing palaces,
Daisy dreams on,

                              WITH A
                                TICKET IN
                                    TATTS!

Good-bye Iceman!

Ladies always standing on the first-floor landing
Ladies in the el-
      e-
        vator,

Ladies, looking, looking, while the
    sausages are cooking,
Looking at the ice in the refrig-
    er-
      ator—
Once there was an Iceman, full of
    burning smirks,
Cupid's Casanova from the freezing
    works;
Now there's only porcelain, cup-
    boards, and duplicity,
Pipes and wheels and switches, and
    stupid electricity,
And girls grow sick of the cold click,
    click
Of the
    New
      Re-
        frig-
          er-
            ator.

And why do you listen, little pink
    lady,
What are you waiting for there all
    day?
Oh, a sigh or a sound from a ghost
    on his round,
And the tramp of a foot far away!

There's the great invention, full of
    condescension,
Waiting like a deaf dumb-
    waiter,
But you don't get passion in any
    sort of fashion
From an up-to-date respectable
    Re-
      frig-
        er-
          ator!

Once there was an Iceman, took us all by storm,
His ice was cold, but his heart was warm,
Now there's only clockwork, motors and thermometers,
Whirligigs in cylinders, and gases in gasometers,
And it isn't half as nice, it's a sneaking sort of ice
    From the
      New
        Re-
          frig-
            er-
              ator!

So listen no longer, little pink lady,
    No one is tramping to knock at your door,
There's no more romance in the iceman's glance,
    And he doesn't come round any more.

Mannequins

Mannequin, mannequin,
  floating up in taffeta,
Dressing up for palaces,
  living in a flat—
"Very, very striking! Cut
  to Madam's liking!"
Says the Ninety Guinea
Model in the
  BIG BLACK HAT.

Up and down in Lanvin, up
  and down in Poiret,
Scornful in the elbow,
  haughty in the eye,
There she goes in bangles,
  there she goes in spangles,
There she goes in beauty
  that a cheque can't buy.

Dowagers in diamonds,
  double chins and lap-
  dogs,
Full of adiposity, cabbages
  and cash—
"Madam would be thinner
  if she went without her
  dinner,"
Says the Champs Elysees
Costume with the
  PINK SILK SASH.

Up and down in Redfern, up
  and down in Paquin,
Curling up her Kissproof,
  tossing up her head;
Petal of the peerage, sniffing
  at the steerage,
  Adding up expenses—sav-
  eloys and bed.

Mannequin, mannequin, going
  home in jitneys,
  Going home in buses to a
  Crown Street flat.
Poverty and squalor—"Lend us
  half-a-dollar!"
  Says the Renovated Model in
  the
    FIVE BOB HAT.

Up and down in Remnants, up
  and down in Greasespots,
  Cutting up potatoes on the
  fourth floor back—
Pie and pickle Clarice, far away
  from Paris,
  Lady Creme de Woolworth's
  frightened of the Sack!

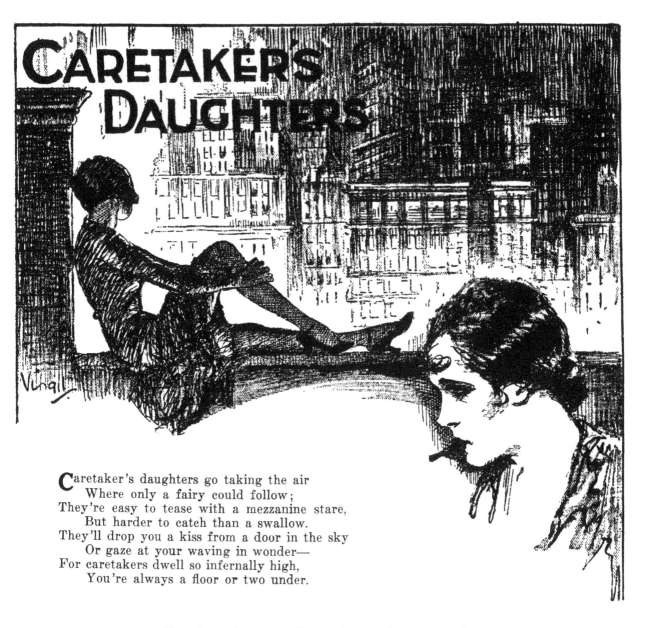

CARETAKER'S DAUGHTERS

Caretaker's daughters go taking the air
    Where only a fairy could follow;
They're easy to tease with a mezzanine stare,
    But harder to catch than a swallow.
They'll drop you a kiss from a door in the sky
    Or gaze at your waving in wonder—
For caretakers dwell so infernally high,
    You're always a floor or two under.

You chase them up ledges and race them up planks,
By parapet-edges and ladders and tanks,
They laugh on the heights, while sore in the hoof
You toil up nine flights to the Girl on the Roof!

Be off with your impudent waving Down There,
    Away with your candy and roses!
You're down in the basement, they're up in the air,
    Or scraping the sky with their noses.
No matter what passion your bosom declares,
    With frenzied affection expanding,
You'll wear out your ankles up 99 stairs,
    Or faint with fatigue on the landing.

For caretaker's quarters are up on
    the roof;
No wonder their daughters are rather
    aloof—
On footing more firm, and with
    notions less high
You wave like a worm at a Girl in
    the Sky!

ELEVEN O'CLOCK

Vingil

Miss What's-Her-Name has van-
        ished like a fairy,
She's left the carbon-copies in a
        heap,
    There are yards of potted Pit-
        man
    Like mysterious works by
        Whitman,
And the Underwood is yawning
    in its sleep.

Poor Miss What's-Her-Name.
    Dear little thing,
Works every morning
    At a big
        gas
            ring.

There's steam round THEM
    Like smoke from a loco—
At eleven a.m.
    She makes
        us
            cocoa!

Miss What's-Her-Name is home again from dancing.
She flops herself exhausted in a chair,
    With a few well-chosen phrases
    She has kicked her shoes to blazes,
And her mother (fifty-seven) combs her hair.
    Poor Miss What's-Her-Name.
        Dear little thing,
    Works every night
        For a rhine-
            stone
                ring;

And supper? Ahem!
    There's a parent in loco.
At eleven p.m.
    MA
        makes
            cocoa!

The Lady in the Lift

Oh, why this constant to-and-fro,
    This frequent bustling to the basement
By men, two Saturdays ago
    Notorious for self-effacement?
And why does Jackson scowl at Jones,
    And Brogan blush at Thompson's notice?
The answer comes in ringing tones—
    We've got a Lady in our Otis!

If you're waiting up on Seven, press the button,
    ring the bell,
She can take you up to Heaven, she can drop
    you down to Hell;
Let the Second Storey sneer at you for boasting
    your affection,
She may pause a while and peer at you—
           STOPPED
           FOR
           INSPECTION.

Such quantities of things to shift,
    Such passengers in mad collision,
Before she came to drive our lift
    Were never seen by human vision.
In vain, to pester her with pearls—
    You musn't only BE, but STAY good—
Such things may do for other girls
    Who drive, perhaps, a Standard
                Waygood.

She will drop you seven storeys, with your
    stomach in the air,
While you contemplate the glories of her
    shoulders and her hair;
You can ask her out to sup, but it won't affect
    her frown—
           UP,
         UP,
She will run you up,
    or she'll take you down.
           DOWN,
             DOWN.

PAY · DAY

Away with your bills and your budgets,
  Pooh, pooh, to your paltry accounts!
A fig for tinned salmon, we're dining with Mammon,
  Inflated with mighty amounts.
We're Astors and Fords and Infantas,
  We sniff at the mob in disgust;
We're elegant houris with diamonds for dowries,
  And twenty-five shillings to bust.

O, honied existence!
  We're bolder than bisons,
Our banknotes outdistance
  The late Jimmy Tyson's;
They talk more together
  Than talkies by Warner,
With dear Mr. Heather-
  shaw's name in the corner.

Let's blow all our bullion at Woolworth's,
  Or laze in the lounge like an earl—
Get thoroughly reckless and pur-
    chase a necklace
  With pearls that might really be
      pearl.
We're off in a cab to Romano's
  With rajahs too haughty to speak—
And nobody guesses that Payday
    Princesses
  Eat kippers the rest of the week.

Conceal your derision,
  Cashiers in your cages,
Nor mock at the vision
  When counting our wages.
It's Heathershaw's heyday,
  So fold 'em up tidy—
There's only one payday
  And that day is Friday!

RESIDENTIAL

Phyllis from the country
    With lips as fresh as
        berries,
Eyes that stare without a
        care,
    And cheeks like cherries.

Up and down the terrace
    Innocently flitting,
Trying scores of funny doors
    To find a "bed and sitting."

Such a nice old lady
    Beckons from the landing—
Rather quaint, and caked with paint,
    But full of understanding.

"Down from Molong, sweet-
    heart?"
    Her voice is calculating.
"Board and bed, I think you
    said?
    "Yes, dear. Do you mind
      waiting?"

A gilt and pimply mirror
    Flaps with a distant glit-
    ter.
Somewhere, far off, there
    sounds a cough,
    And somewhere close, **a**
    titter.

CUCUMBER KITTY

When Cucumber Kitty comes mocking the city,
    The boulevards burst into bud,
The dusty old alleys breathe Roger and Gallet's
    And daffodils blaze in the mud.
We dodder and damn on the back of a tram,
    Or burn off the skin from our noses—
But Cucumber Kitty, without any pity,
    Goes flagrantly,
    Vagrantly,
        Floating so fragrantly,
    Cooler than Eskimo roses.

And why does she never get sunstroke
    In such an inadequate hat?
If you beg for advice, she will recommend ice,
    But you know very well it's not THAT!

Oh, pull up the shutters, there's tar in the gutters!
    Oh, turn on the punkahs, and doze;
We're stupid and sticky with heat and gin-rickey,
    But look! I'll be hanged! There she goes!

Let the westerlies roar, they afflict her no more
    Than a bath-heater worries a plumber—
It's Cucumber Kitty, so cool and so pretty.
    So airily,
    Warily,
        Lightly and merrily,
    Snapping her fingers at summer!

Don't bother to ask me the secret,
    The answer is buried in heat—
I'm satisfied now to sit dabbing my brow
    While she ices my side of the street!

The Beauty Parlor!

She has Venus in a bottle, and beauty in a jar,
  She can turn a little typist to a motion-picture
      star,
    She can dazzle with her science
    All varieties of clients
From the semi-Oriental to the elegant bizarre.

Does your boy-friend love to touch you? Let us have
  a little chat.
Is your chin, alas, too plural? She can give you things
  for that,
    Or a recipe for henna
      From a "countess in Vienna,"
Or a course of 15 treatments for the discontented fat.

She can tell you full particulars
  of Mr. Cohen's yacht,
Why he went to Middle Harbor, whom
  he took with him and what;
All the interesting orgies
  Of the Johnnies and the Georgies,
She will hand you with the cold cream
  in a whisper or a pot.

She's got "secrets of society" displayed
  upon the shelf,
All the beautifying balms of Lady An
  gelina Guelph—
  Though she has them by the gallon,
  Madame Sophie of "The Salon"
(You will notice from the picture)
  doesn't use them on herself

UNDERGROUND ROSES

You can talk of botanical gardens,
  Where roses are commonly found,
But the kind that I mean are less frequently seen—
  They're the roses that grow underground.
In the caverns of thundering marble,
  They bloom at 8.30 a.m.,
Or they hang by a door to the 5.44
  As a tiger-rose hangs to the stem.

Underground Roses, powdering noses, down where the sirens
      moo,
Cherubs in chokers, clinging to smokers, rushing the Rockdale
    Through;
Giggles and kisses and Black Narcissus, gurgles and gossip
    and glee,
Like buried canaries, the underground fairies go carolling
    home to tea!

  "Museum! Museum! Museum!"
    The passionate porter exclaims—
At a smile from a Rose he forgets all he knows,
    And goes mixing it up with St. James.
The Queen is aghast on her statue
    At such a delectable view,
But the Saint, with a sigh, turns away from the sky,
    And would like to go underground, too!

Who wouldn't suffer a ride on a buffer to talk to an
      Underground Rose?
Clerks without pity embark for the city and trample
    all over her toes;
Underground ladies, like angels in Hades, the
    Roses that Never Sit Down,
              With pink little faces
              and vanity cases, go
              scampering back into
              town!

The Gunman's Girl

The gunman's girl wears mother-of-pearl
　And a coat of real oppossum;
With a face like stone she walks alone
　In a land where the Snowdrops blossom.
There's a kiss of a knife on her neck for
　life,
　And a diamond (the latest fashion).
For bruises and bangles are mixed in
　tangles
　When a gunman bends to passion.

And, O, beware when she takes the air,
　Take care in the streets at night—
Cross over and hide on the opposite side
　To Dangerous Dan's delight—
So give her a cautious peep, my lad,
　From the edge of a hang-dog eye
When a Smith & Wesson delicatessen
　Gunman's girl goes by!

O, what are they at in the gun
　man's flat?
　My friend you are quite mis-
　taken.
One peep behind, and you'll
　probably find
　She's cooking him eggs and
　bacon.
Professional hours in bad men's
　bowers
　Are all very well for rookery,
　But a gunman's wife in private
　life
　Is more concerned with cookery

And, O, beware when she takes
　the air,
　Take care in the streets at
　night—
She's wheeling a pram with a
　pound of ham
　For a bad man's appetite
She's carrying butter and eggs,
　my lad,
　There's bacon at home to fry,
　When the Smith & Wesson
　delicatessen
　Gunman's girl goes by!

The Girl at the Wheel

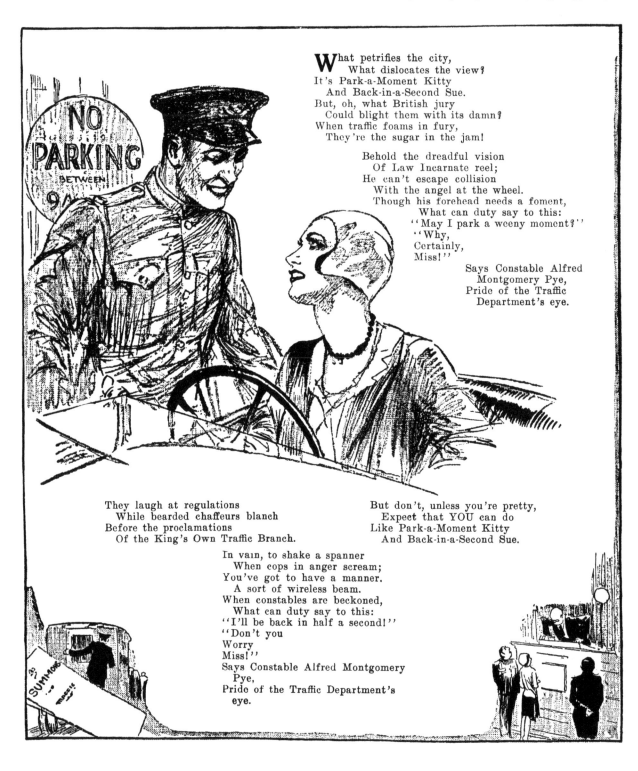

What petrifies the city,
  What dislocates the view?
It's Park-a-Moment Kitty
  And Back-in-a-Second Sue.
But, oh, what British jury
  Could blight them with its damn?
When traffic foams in fury,
  They're the sugar in the jam!

Behold the dreadful vision
  Of Law Incarnate reel;
He can't escape collision
  With the angel at the wheel.
Though his forehead needs a foment,
  What can duty say to this:
"May I park a weeny moment?"
"Why,
  Certainly,
    Miss!"

Says Constable Alfred
  Montgomery Pye,
Pride of the Traffic
  Department's eye.

They laugh at regulations
  While bearded chauffeurs blanch
Before the proclamations
  Of the King's Own Traffic Branch.

In vain, to shake a spanner
  When cops in anger scream;
You've got to have a manner.
  A sort of wireless beam.
When constables are beckoned,
  What can duty say to this:
"I'll be back in half a second!"
"Don't you
  Worry
    Miss!"
Says Constable Alfred Montgomery
  Pye,
Pride of the Traffic Department's
  eye.

But don't, unless you're pretty,
  Expect that YOU can do
Like Park-a-Moment Kitty
  And Back-in-a-Second Sue.

Going Home

It's nice to know a fellow with a fancy for a Yellow;
  It's nice and all, I quite agree,
For them with diamond brooches to ride in Marmon coaches,
  But what I says is,
    Trams
      Do
        Me.
It don't take a brush like Orpen's
  To depict the dashing scene
When I pays me frugal fourpence
  On the 5.15.,
It don't need a Michael Arlen
  To describe it if he cquld—
But it's trams, me little darlin',
  Keep a
    GOOD
      girl
      GOOD.
It's easy to disparage the discomfort of the carriage,
  And the fare may be accounted as a loss,
But I'd sooner sit and suffer on a footboard or a
    buffer
  Than risk it in a taxi
    with
      the
        boss.
There are blondes who pass St. Mary's
  In a manner that is free,
But I don't believe in fairies,
  And a tram does me;
So I stands and holds me money
  Where I've very often stood,
For it's trams, believe me, honey,
  Keep a
    GOOD
      girl
      GOOD.

TETE·A·TETE

SIGNORA DEL UNDERWOOD, greeting!
  Behold me, a ninepenny host!
Forget this inferno of eating,
    These gluttons of hot-buttered toast;
They gabble and gobble and garble,
  But we're in a world of our own—
This table, observe, is real marble,
    This chair—pray be seated—a throne.

      Some chicken in curry, Contessa?
      Ho, garcon, la! Hurry! A plate!
      I'm a hell of a sheik, I get £5 a week,
      But who thinks of that, tete-a-tete,
        Tete-a-tete,
      Side by side, cheek by cheek,
        Tete-a-tete?

Oh, please don't address me as "Horace,"
  It's something I want to forget—
Imagine you're dining with MAURICE,
    And you (let us say) are JEANNETTE.
And Pitt Street is part of the Lido
  Where princes eat partridge and ham,
And 95 miles on the speedo
    Is better than taking a tram.

      A trifle more truffle, Marchesa?
      The waiters all scuffle to wait;
      They're dukes in disguise, rolling Romanoff eyes,
      But what do we care, tete-a-tete,
        Tete-a-tete?
      (Cup of tea and two pies,
        Tete-a-tete).

      Romano himself comes appealing
        (Two pies, cup of tea, deener each),
      The moon kind of drips through the ceiling,
        The waves are like wine on the beach.
      Behold my Hispano-Suiza!
        Would Madam come out for a dance?
      Then pick up your diamonds, Teresa,
        And give Mr. Menjou a chance!

Some more Maraschino,
    Princessa?
Allow me! Casinos can
    wait;
They can charge one and
    three for a third cup
    of tea,
But damn the expense, tete-
    a-tete,
    Tete-a-tete,
(Let's walk to the Quay
    Tete-a-tete!)

SERENADE

Oh, virgins in tropical villas,
  Come hark to my Spanish guitar;
You ladies with tango mantillas
  Who dwell in the flats "Alcazar,"
Those pretty pink sarsaparillary
Concoctions of dreams and distillery
With fountains and fishponds and frillery
  And tiles more bizonk than bizarre.

    Plink-a-plink, plink-a-plink,
    Bits of glass, bits of zinc,
    And tiles more bizonk than bizarre.

Though Carmens incessantly vanish,
  And damsels with hurricane-hair
Are not necessarily Spanish—
  At least, be as daft as you dare.
Fair blossoms who scorn macaroni—oh
Ye that adorn "San Antonio"
Disguise your connection with Roneo
  When taking up residence there.

    Plink-a-plank, plink-a-plank,
    You may work in a bank,
    But please not to mention it there.

Can this be El Duque who proposes?
  Imagine it is, if you can—
But you should be firing down roses
  Or bashfully biting a fan,
And I should be christened Ignacio
Fernando Come-into-the-Patio
Porfirio Flor del Moustachio
  de las Cruzes y Jaime Esteban.

    Plink-a-plonk, plink-a-plonk,
    This may sound pretty cronk,
    But it's better than HECTOR or DAN.

And do you adore "La Paloma,"
  Wear roses behind the left ear
Or dote in a species of coma
  At solos on bones? No damn fear.
You turn with a sneer to your savoury.
Adjusting your permanent wavery,
And nobody thinks of my bravery
  In singing a serenade here

    Plink-a-plunk, plink-a-plunk,
    "What a nuisance! He's drunk,
    But he will insist coming round here!"

The Night Express

Out of the night, immense and shrill,
   It comes with cloudy fire
To curse a girl at Bogan's Hill
   With torments of desire.
A string of golden window-lights,
   A rope of flame—they've gone.
Over the windy mountain-heights,
   The night-express flies on.

Drowned in the silent loneliness,
   The lantern's ruby dies.
A girl looks at the night-express
   With bright and wistful eyes.
The night-express, with panther grace,
   On reaching Bogan's Hill,
Shows its opinion of the place
   By going faster still.

O, to be on the night-express
   O, to be there some day,
Miles to go with a port-mant-eau
   And a ticket for far away!

The Pullman cars are full of light,
   And lurching corridors,
And swagmen huddled out of sight,
   And cigarettes and snores,
The atmosphere you find on trains,
   And fat men playing cards,
And tumbling jugs and rattling panes
   And honeymoons and guards.

The engine roars, the whistle cries,
   The echoes follow shrill;
A girl sits on her berth, and sighs,
   And stares at Bogan's Hill.
Pulling the window-blind, she sees
   A moment into space—
A shed, a flash of moonlit trees,
   Some milk tins and a face.

And, O, to be in Bogan's Hill.
   O, to be there some day,
Cows and peace—release, release,
   And the night-express far away!

THE VESTIBULE

In caverns of marble
  With candle and bell,
Its gossip to garble,
  Its tattle to tell,
Its trouble to cheer,
  Its hurry to cool
The world waits here
  In the Vest-i-bule.

With fortunes and fables
  And pageboys and plots,
And luggage with labels
  From Shepheard's to Scott's.
Adventurer, spy,
  Madonna and fool,
They all pass by
  In the Vest-i-bule.

Fairy princesses
  With cherry pink lips,
And trunks full of dresses
  And hands full of tips,
And angels and thieves,
  And blossoms from school,
Brushing their sleeves
  In the Vest-i-bule.

But someday they'll muffle
  Their laughter and bells,
For Death doesn't shuffle
  His pick of hotels;
The waiters don't know,
  They're dumb as a rule—
BUT WHERE DO WE GO
  FROM THE VEST-I-BULE?

Miss Pillion.

When curls were done in a golden bun
 And whiskers grew by the million,
You'd frequently find a girl behind
 On the good old country pillion.
With a blush and a murmur, she'd wriggle up firmer
 (Which some thought grounds for divorce),
"There's What's-His-Name! I shall die of shame!"
  Said the Girl
    On the Back
      Of the Horse.

Where Uncle James with his bygone flames
 On a bob-tailed nag would canter,
His niece goes out on an Indian Scout
 In a lavender tam-o'-shanter.
There's a bang and a scatter and a headlong
  clatter
 And a roar in the middle of the track—
"Oh, scowl if you must, but pardon our
  dust!"
 Says the Girl
   On the Bike
     At the Back.

Let Pa explode on the Canterbury Road
 And Grandpa write to the paper,
She'll sit all day on a B.S.A.
 In the usual cloud of vapor.
You can gaze at her giddily from your
  Armstrong-Siddeley.
 You can frown at the hussy if you like.
"Let her out, old fruit! Cheerio, toot-
  toot!"
 Says the Girl
   On the Back
     Of the Bike.

SNOWDROPS

The Snowdrop Girl in fields of
  snowdrops walks,
Whiter than foam, deeper than
  waters flowing,
Flakes of wild milk gone blowing,
Snowing on cloudy stalks.
The Snowdrop Girl goes picking
  flowers of snow,
Blossoms of darkness bubbling into
  dreams,
In a strange country, by the shadowy
  streams
Where the cruel petals of the Coke-
  Tree grow.

From the smoke and the fume of a
  backyard room,
  Where poverty sits and gloats,
On runaway feet from a dirty street
  To a field of snow she floats;
And tickets to hell have a curious
  smell
  And a dangerous crystal whiff,
Where men hawk Death in a snow-
  drop's breath
  At a couple of shillings a sniff.

The Snowdrop Girl in fields of snowdrops dwells,
Whiter than graveyard stones, whiter than crosses;
Over her sleep there tosses
A wilderness of bells.
Oh, Snowdrop Girl, picking your blossoms here,
The road grows dark and bitter further on
Where other, lonelier Snowdrop Girls have gone,
Lost in the poisoned snows of yesteryear.
Beware, beware, those petals of air—
  There's never a flower in slums.
You're caught in a cage on the basic wage,
  But wait till the Snowman comes!
Then the arclights blaze as you walk in a daze,
  And the hags of the pavement grin,
And Snow, no doubt, may let you out,
  But the grave will suck you in!

THE ROAD TO MANDOLIN

Once in the heyday of ringlets,
  Cupid was frequently seen
Trying on calico singlets,
  Out of regard for the Queen.
Lutes were no longer in fashion,
  Kisses were numbered with sins,
Cupid, when bending to passion,
  Always preferred mandolins,
    Plink-a-plink,
  Always preferred mandolins.

Maidens adored mandolins then,
  Teaching their lovers to strum.
But now they demand a saxophone band,
  Five trumpets, a trombone and drum.

Parlors with busts of Disraeli
  Echoed that wistful refrain,
Notes that the cheap ukulele
  Hopelessly seeks to regain.
Grandpa, most patient of students,
  Sat with his hand on his chin,
Preening his whiskers while Prudence
  Played him the gay mandolin,
    Prink-a-prink,
  Played him the gay mandolin.
But maidens don't strum mandolins now,
  And lovers don't listen in bliss.
All they play, with a laugh, is a tin
    phonograph,
  And it doesn't take much to play this.

Damsels, to gladden a hero,
  Gorgeous in trousers of plaid,
  Played him "The Gay Bandolero"—
  "Devilish fetching, by gad!"—
But flappers prefer the piano,
  And dancers insist on a din,
And down in the vaults of Romano
  You won't hear the gay mandolin,
    Plink-a-plonk,
  You won't hear the gay mandolin.
No, maidens don't do it like that now,
  The mandolin's fallen asleep.
    It's Lot 34 in a furniture
        store—
    "This Musical Instru-
        ment, Cheap."

In A/C with Ghosts

You can shuffle and scuffle and scold,
  You can rattle the knockers and knobs,
Or batter the doorsteps with buckets of gold
  Till the Deputy-Governor sobs.
You can sneak up a suitable plank
  In a frantic endeavor to see—
But what do they do in the Commonwealth Bank
  When the Big Door bangs at Three?

Listen in the cellars, listen in the vaults,
Can't you hear the tellers turning somersaults?
Can't you hear the spectres of inspectors and
    directors
Dancing with the phantoms in a Dead Man's
    Waltz?
Some are ghosts of nabobs, poverty and stray
    bobs,
Midas and his mistress, Mammon and his wife;
Other ones are sentries, guarding double entries,

Long-forgotten, double-dealing, troubled double-
    life.
Down among the pass-books, money lent and
    spent,
Down among the forests of the Four Per Cent.,
Where the ledgers meet and moulder, and the
    overdrafts grow older,
And the phantoms shrug a shoulder when you
    ask 'em for the rent.

They are bogies of Grandfather's cheques,
  They are spectres of buried accounts,
They are crinoline sweethearts with pearls on
    their necks,
  Demanding enormous amounts.
They are payment for suppers and flowers,
  For diamonds to banish a tear,
For sweet, pretty ladies in opulent hours . . .
  And tombstones . . . and bailiffs . . . and
    beer . . . .

Down in the bowels of the bank, the ledgers lie
    rank upon rank,
The debts of the ages come out of their pages,
The bones of old loans creak and clank—
Oh, if you could peep through the door
To-day at a Quarter Past Four,
You'd find all the ghosts at their usual posts,
    And you wouldn't
      sign cheques
        any more!

Mademoiselle—All of Them

She's blonde and petite, she's dark and discreet,
  She's plump, and uncommonly slender.
Her eyes get you down, they're purple—no, brown.
  Her smile is both mocking and tender.
She's frozen and fair, with buttercup hair;
  She's brown as a berry, and shingled.
I can picture her yet, just a red-haired brunette,
  With a touch of the Orient mingled.

  Mademoiselle from Armentieres,
    The Diggers will argue about her for years.
    If you trust them all, and you haven't gone deaf,
    She was kissed by the whole flaming A.I.F.

According to Jim, she's remarkably slim;
  According to Steve she is tubby.
Both Henry and Dick thought she looked rather sick,
  But William describes her as chubby.
She changes her face to accord with each case,
  She matches the fancy of Nigger—
In fact, it would seem, she was only a dream,
  But a dream that was dear to the Digger.

Mademoiselle from Armentieres,
Pride of the tanks and the engineers,
    —and the pioneers,
    —and the brigadiers,
    —and the grenadiers,
    —and the fusiliers,
    —and the bombardiers,
    —and the volunteers,
Mademoiselle from
    Armentieres!

LONELY

I'd like to buy some singing-birds,
  And strings of golden jade,
And floppy books with tender words
  In sentimental suede,
I'd like to buy some roller skates,
  I'd like to buy some cartridges,
And piles of willow-pattern plates,
  And half-a-dozen partridges.

I would love to send a guinea to my little sister
    Winnie,
If I had a little Winnie, BUT I'M LONELY!
And a rustless steel stiletto to my uncle in the
    Ghetto,
  If I had a sort of uncle, BUT I'M LONELY!
I would give my cousin Gerald a subscription to the
    "Herald"
Or a model of a schooner, or a little thing by Gruner
And a step-sister at Pymble an electroplated thimble
And devoted Great-aunt Dinah, doing uplift work
    in China,
I'd remember with some kisses, and a pot of Black
    Narcissus,
Or a bangle, or a ribbon, or the works of Edward
    Gibbon,
        IF I'D ONLY
Got a cousin or a great-aunt, or a pal at Parramatta,
Or a lubra at Maroubra, or a boy in Wangaratta,
But I'm lonely,
          lonely,
              lonely!

The papers bang their tambourine:
  "Give Him a trouser-press!"
"Give Them a poker-work machine!"
  "Give Her a satin dress!"
I feel I'd like to please the whim,
  And buy a pretty fur,
But, oh, I don't possess a Him,
  I haven't got a Her!

Coty's crystals, water-pistols, mandolins, and mer-
    cery,
Something for the motor car and something for the
    nursery,
Cigarettes and novelettes and phonographs and tri-
    cycles,
Yards and yards of Christmas cards with mistletoe
    and icicles,
All the girls are buying them, and wrapping them,
    and sending them,
Every girl has got her friends, but never thinks of
    lending them,
All the windows shine with things for Other People
    Only,
All the world is kissing, and I'm lonely,
                lonely,
                  lonely!

EVOLUTION

Oh, barbarous, beautiful girl
  Carousing to 'Little White Lies,''
With a wave in each flyaway curl
  And a beckon in both of your eyes,
Do you think you're so frightfully slinky,
  So timed-to-the-tick '31,
Because, little monkey, your furs are so minky,
Your drinks are so pinky, your coupe so dinky,
  And dancing such fun?

The dinosaur's den you forget,
  Romano's gay caverns you crave;
But it isn't so long since we met
  In another description of cave.
Your chin had a chic Talgai angle,
  You didn't wear very much less—
It's rather a bungle to put on a bangle,
Two shoes and a spangle, where leaves used to dangle
  Instead of a dress.

And years before THAT, we had swung
  Through jungles long crumbled to shale,
While you, perhaps, girlishly hung
  By the tip of your sweet pretty tail;
And years before THAT, we were fishes
  In some sort of primitive bog;
Or, bounding in dishes, I carried choice dishes
To you—a capricious, entirely delicious
  Young womanly frog.

Ah, let us not mention it here,
  Nor follow the trail any more,
When you were a tadpole, my dear,
  And I was a toad on the shore.
Give thanks to the queer bit of jelly
  That swam in a far-away sea,
And turned willy-nilly to Nancy and Nelly
And Marie Corelli and Lang and Ned Kelly and YOU,
  Yes, and ME!

THE SNOW MAIDEN

Down where the ducks wear gaiters,
　　Down where the icebergs clink,
Colder than Kelvinators,
　　Bleak as a barmaid's wink,
Iced like an iceman's daughter,
　　Laughing at five degrees,
Daphne goes down to the water,
　　Bidding the sea-gulls freeze.

If you don't believe it, you've only got
　　to wait,
Peep through the window at half-past
　　eight;
The ice goes clink, but she doesn't give
　　a rap,
In her cherry-pink costume with the
　　little Green Cap.

Far from the surf-club hero
　　Hugging his knees in bed,
Down in the depths of Zero,
　　Daphne is miles ahead,
Dodging a deep-sea breaker,
　　Perched on a frozen shoot,
Cold as an undertaker
　　Firing a funeral mute.

If you don't believe it, blow away the
　　dew,
Peer through the window, shudder at
　　the view;
Pull down the bed-clothes, take another
　　nap—
Far away out bobs the little Green Cap.

Show her an ocean chillier,
　　Cooled by a Frigidaire,
Stern as the ice of Hillier,
　　Daphne would dive in there,
Frisk with a frozen dumper,
　　Follow the penguins through—
If only below her jumper
　　Her blood were not frozen too!

If you don't believe it, and you won't be told,
Have a conversation. Boy, this girl is cold!
Your heart might break, and she wouldn't care a scrap,
In her cherry-pink costume with the little Green Cap.

The Ballad of the Knee

When Cupid was coy and complacent,
 And garters were harder to see,
We guessed you were somewhere adjacent,
 But didn't confess it, O Knee!
With many a bombazine button,
 With many a taffeta pleat,
In sleeves of historical mutton,
 Our mothers were born without feet.

To-day they possess no objection
 To flaunting patellas at men,
And knees are as free for inspection
 As antimacassars were then.
But somehow the magic has faded,
 The glamour has gone from the air,
And critics are almost persuaded
 That knees aren't as good as they were.

Oh, come back to black satin bustles,
 And whiskers where sparrows laid eggs,
When Pa tried to smarten his trousers with
 tartan,
 And ladies walked out without legs!

Oh, come back to parrots and peignoirs,
 And petticoats buried from view,
When men in Dundrearies were tortured
 with queries
At seeing a little pink shoe.

When fugitive ankles of Phoebes
 Were bared in the wicked gavotte,
Our fathers contracted the Jeebies,
 And some would go blind on the spot.
But where is that simple emotion,
 And where have the Jeebies gone now,
When knees are like fish in the ocean
 And garters hang wild on the bough?

Oh, come back to nightcaps and flannel,
 Come back to the flounce and the frill,
When flappers in satin consumed no Manhattan,
 And knees could still give us a thrill!

44

The All-Night Taxi Stand

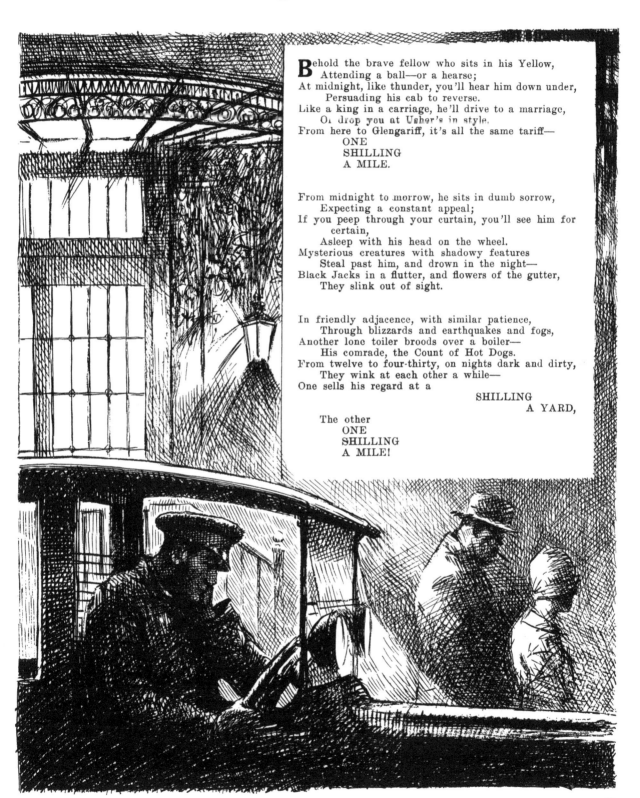

Behold the brave fellow who sits in his Yellow,
  Attending a ball—or a hearse;
At midnight, like thunder, you'll hear him down under,
  Persuading his cab to reverse.
Like a king in a carriage, he'll drive to a marriage,
  Or drop you at Usher's in style.
From here to Glengariff, it's all the same tariff—
    ONE
    SHILLING
    A MILE.

From midnight to morrow, he sits in dumb sorrow,
  Expecting a constant appeal;
If you peep through your curtain, you'll see him for
    certain,
  Asleep with his head on the wheel.
Mysterious creatures with shadowy features
  Steal past him, and drown in the night—
Black Jacks in a flutter, and flowers of the gutter,
  They slink out of sight.

In friendly adjacence, with similar patience,
  Through blizzards and earthquakes and fogs,
Another lone toiler broods over a boiler—
  His comrade, the Count of Hot Dogs.
From twelve to four-thirty, on nights dark and dirty,
  They wink at each other a while—
One sells his regard at a
                SHILLING
                    A YARD,

    The other
      ONE
      SHILLING
      A MILE!

Good~bye—Chorus Lady!

Ankles that answered our clapping,
   Limbs that rotated like one,
Where do your slippers go tapping
   Now that the chorus is done?
Nobody waits in a Yellow,
   Bribing the doorkeeper's growls—
Only the Vitaphones bellow,
   Only the Magnavox howls.

Daisy de Vere (nee Maloney),
   Rosie, the poet's delight,
Susie, my pantomime pony—
   Where are you dancing to-night?
Shadows have plundered your flattery,
   Phantoms have stolen your hire—
Legs that come out of a battery,
   Voices that cry through a wire.

Daisy who danced for us, danced for us,
   Danced in her cherry-pink tights;
Rosie who sang for us, sang for us,
   Sang like a bird from the heights;
And Susie (ah, Susie!) who didn't do nothing
   But walk up a staircase on Saturday
      nights. . . .

Never again will the love-stricken super
Gloat from the wings in beatified stupor,
Never again will the pink feet whirl . . .
And you can't make dates with a Paramount
   girl!

Daisy is dancing, is dancing
   Attendance while shop-walkers sign,
A kind of unwilling, thirty-five shilling,
   Corset-department's Columbine;
Rosie is singing, is singing
   Out orders from seven to nine,
Wasting her legs on bacon and eggs,
   And buckets of soup and bottles of wine;
And Susie (ah, Susie!) is acting
   As though she had money to dine,
Feasting on air with water-waved hair
   And nails there is plenty of leisure to
      shine.

But nobody waits in Chrysanthemum Alley
For the Western Electric corps-de-ballet,
And nobody listens, and nobody knocks,
With a bunch of flowers for a Magnavox!

Printed in Australia
Ingram Content Group Australia Pty Ltd
AUHW010947131124
402703AU00005B/12